Connections

Jennefer York Cole

ISBN: 978-93-6354-374-4

First Edition: 2026
Rs. 200/-

Cyberwit.net
HIG 45 Kaushambi Kunj, Kalindipuram
Allahabad - 211011 (U.P.) India
http://www.cyberwit.net
E-mail: info@cyberwit.net

Printed at Vcore.

To the girls and Rob as always.

Acknowledgements:

I would like to thank the editors of the following publications in which some of these poems, or earlier versions of them, appear:

The Broadkill Review
FLAR (Fredericksburg Literary and Art Review)
Erbacce Press
Addanomadd
Ink, Sweat, and Tears

I would also like to thank the Poetry Society's Stanza Crit Group France for all their helpful feedback over the years. It has been a great adventure!

These poems are a collection of works written over the last 6 years following the deaths of my mother and then my husband. The act of writing helped me through the grieving process, still helps me, and I hope that they will help anyone who can connect with the ideas brought out.

Contents

I. Mother/Father connections....

Spring Cleaning

Clearing out a cupboard reveals teeth
in a box like sacred relics, old baby

bones, broken and cracked
with age. Hoary wives whisper *Bury*

them in the garden… and so what
will grow? The time has passed,

since your toothy 3-year-old smile
at a streetlight answered my request

to feel soft flesh, warm and pliable
to touch, a hand I made from scratch,

in my own. Your No a shock, stopped
me dead in my tracks. *Why? Because,*

you insisted. You had already enclosed
something else in empty fists & moved on,

exposing a world in your mind with no door
for me to wander through, have a look,

sit for a while, ponder my place. Baby
teeth fill my palm - a past part of you

like a missing link - the gaps, now straightened
caries, wisdoms extracted fourfold. They leave

me queasy yet captivated by the vastness
of those minute vacant spaces.

Tiny Dancers

i.

It's bikini season again
though the one piece is
trending like in '91 &
summer camp initiation.

In a mall with cozy armchairs,
and colorful racks, Mom showed
me suitable ones with padded
bras for nipple-less breasts

lest any gaze be tempted. I found
mine, little corseted waist, forced
it on again at home in front of dad
for his awkward approval;

walking back and forth, in a
balancé movement, spinning
on my heel, a boxed jewelry
dancer, tiny arms raised high.

ii.

Now a tumor walks across
his throat growing limbs
that wrap around the nerves,

arms reaching out, hands
waving like goodbye,
& tiny clotted words on
my tongue leave me
no response while my mind
reels & walks away.

iii.

It's bikini season again
that ritual peeling down

through layers to exposed
skin. I was 13, learning

to shave, balanced on
wet camp tiles other feet

had touched before, knee bent,
in a frontal *attitude*,

an exotic bird dancing
when my hand slipped,

nicked the ankle bone -
mingled blood to water

washing everything down
the drain except a scab, &

a tiny scar that remains
to remember, drying off

at the poolside, knee bent,
wet leg balanced out.

iv.

I took Mom back home, in part,
surreptitiously in a glass jar,
remains of her I could have pieced
together to mother myself. We
walked around the town's walled
waterway & as dad talked about
the best way to maneuver this task,
I tipped her all out, surprising us both.
She formed a cloud under the surface;
in a slow, ash-white *adagio*,
& bubbles floated up
like expelled breath when she laid down
on the riverbed to rest, surprising us both.

v.

It's bikini season again –
though this year is nothing
like we imagined last time –

& I dream of warm
pooled skin or salty air
on my tongue & you, my own

tiny dancer, are scared
though there is nothing to fear
here in this little bedded space

where you will not remember
what I say. That serpent
you seem to dream of is not real

nor the water it dances in
nor the wrist it wraps around
in a *pirouette* over your clenched

fist & not even this woman -
who you cannot see -
who comes in darkness to soothe.

Foreign Objects, 1974

I.
I guess it was decided in the bath.
Gone home to tidy up before
we came over, it must have been
then my mother said, *No, not yet.*
Naked in a warm water *caresse*
when the neighbor walked in
par accident. Their eyes met over
her breasts and connected.
Without us kids. It seems we
didn't fit the picture: that still
surface, her trapped reflection.
And so we were left outside
love's closed doors watching
ripples flashing on wood.

II.
Nobody knows precisely when she died.
Her key was lost, they broke the door
and found her, heart turned off
across the sofa, in a sea of debris:
papers and cigarettes and packs
of chips left at her feet. *Mon dieu,*
I thought, 'till Mr. Mercier,
ex machina, came to empty house.
An old *Pied Noir,* a magical misfit,
he waded through the mess my mother
left behind. To him her rooms revealed
their worth. He cleared the way and fell

in love with a portrait I'd always thought
off kilter – her younger face, staring out.

III.
Between us, an ocean *et deux*
langues got in the way but here,
framed snap shots of my face's
past stages stare back at me.
Mieux vaut l'avoir en photo.
I know it is anger not grief
that drowns out my senses.
Her fear of touch I could
not grasp. Now you hold open
the bag for me and sweep up
dated and annotated, dried out
papers, piled dead leaves
in the corner, while I thumb
through recent bank statements.

Foreign Objects, 2019

I.
Just lay back and relax, feet up,
you'll feel the cool instrument, some
pressure, and a slight scraping inside.
I try to ignore the Dr's hands,
never easier with time, & my
mother's voice tickles my ear from
last time we met (before her ashes
filled a lily stamped cardboard tube)
telling guests *ma fille est belle, inside*
and out, as she lit another cigarette.
Yet how could she know?
I cannot see in her expired eyes
my reversed image; can only feel
cold steel & sheets that crinkle.

II.
I took my daughter for her first
visit a year ago, wanted to explain
the procedure beforehand to ease
her fears and remembered rear-view
white-clad blonds settled in a row
in the back seat, whispering about
nos marguerites, with me slowly
understanding the subject wasn't
daisies. So in the waiting room,
turning dusty, worn out pages,
I used no euphemism as cover

but you have to feel it to know
that scratch deep inside. Was it
cruel to speak of cold, hard truths?

III.
I dug down into the lily printed
cylinder, dust floated in the air,
settled on my hand: mother & daughter
combined *juste pour un instant.*
A covert jam jar full of her, in part,
to smuggle overseas. Now my arms
rest on the railing of the bridge
with feet firmly planted on pavement
as drunks cry out to toss a dime or two.
I throw her over the edge with a wish,
in that city she loved more than me.
No longer hard, I examine her beauty
in the cold as she catches the light,
reflecting, and falls *tout doucement.*

States of Matter

Steam carries scents of cotton and old sweat
up to my nose as I iron. Ice melts
in my drink, completes three states of changing
matter. His voice flows from an empty chair
with attempts at Shakespeare trying to be
(or not) a high school lesson plan. Gardens
and balconies and donkey heads transformed
summer days into enchanted moments:
suggestions made on how to entertain
teens before hall bells rang time to a close.
Dad paid me 50 cents a shirt for starch
and an unformed opinion. I still think
he wanted to share somehow. Now his shirts,
in piles, fill up bags for the Goodwill.

Our Kitchen Table (2020)

I look over at the spot and think of the word spot. It’s so easy to go from *spot on* to *a spot of bother*. It comes from Old English, *splott* meaning plot of land, like a territory to conquer. Through time it went from *hit the spot*, to be *on the spot*, from things you notice, to a stain on that favorite shirt, now a permanent mark like dotted blemishes on skin. From simply a faithful dog with a waggly tail, to an open space you might want to slip into. A space that could be dark and deep, outer and weightless, or minute, a keyboard bar in the digital world, yet always void. My mind goes through these meanings but there is no connection here between all of this. I look at your empty space, and see one glass, one spoon, one dish.

II. Lover/Partner connections…

Connections

Evening arrived, found me inside the bathroom on
the hard tile floor connected to the outside world
by a receiver and a long rubber cord escaping under
the door from around my younger finger.

I wound, unwound,
and rewound the wire; and the timer ticked down as lines
formed to be next. *Darling. Love. You are the only one.*
Calling voices caressed my ear, words whispered kept,

now
folded pieces of paper in an old perfume box tied
tight with black string at the back of my underwear drawer;
hidden beneath little lacy, grown-up numbers.

And you study wires.
One blue, one brown, to ground the new light
over the toilet in our bathroom. I pass you the clippers
to cut the cords and hold the ladder steady as we talk
about which picture frames to hang on the walls.

The Picnic

We head over to the water thinking
it will cool us down. A quick picnic
along the shore to make life easy,
it's too hot and heavy to cook.

The bugs are bad – it was the wrong
time to come, but we walk on. I talk
and you wait your turn to speak. Did you
remember to bring the knives and forks?

The bright sky squints my eyes, knits my brow,
and you think I'm angry, but I am only
overwhelmed. I've said the wrong thing
again. My words won't express my intent.

A mosquito lands on your cheek, on that soft
edge hidden beneath the three-day stubble.
I try to brush it off to save you from the bite
and leave a lingering trail of blood.

Disaster Dreams

"Everyone carries a shadow, and the less it is embodied in the individual's conscience life, the denser and blacker it is." Jung

Last night, disaster hit again.
Waves crashed over and over,
hitting the shore where I stood,
feet running and running, yet still.
Out there sirens sounded
police coming to find the body
I had hidden underground
in our backyard, piece by piece,
under layers of dirt covering up
what I did. Then the house caught fire,
and the wooden floor caved in
under my feet. My arms would not lift
me, cement wings, to fly to you,
as my hand clutched your shoulder
and rolled you over, your steady breath.
With pounding heart, gulping air,
I rise, wide-eyed, stumble over memories
of revival meetings, bible bashing folk
screaming about fire and brimstone
hands raised high to grasp the truth
and walk away, sleep gone from feet
slapping cold tiles in the corridor.

Dr J.K. and Mr Hide

A volcano erupts
in the kitchen
at the slightest trifle.

A key misplaced.
A glass shattered.
A text fucked up and
sent astray.

Objects slam
with a tremble, and then,
the spewing forth of
molten lava words

strong enough to
peel paint from walls,
melt ears like candle wax,

and turn warm hearts cold.
Passing through lips
that encircle my
nipples
in a holy vow.

Over a tongue
that traces
love letters
across my skin,

my body
held in hands,
so tenderly,
for fear it might
turn to ash
and disappear
in a breath of wind.

I want to
unlock your fingers
with a touch
and watch a fist become
a hand again -
metamorphosis.

Turn over the palm,
angled so I can see
clearly

to read the lines
intertwined.
What is your story?
Where does your
rage reside?

Come lay beside me.
Let me dig down
through your layers
and find
where your fire
and brimstone hide.

Tall Tales

These are the tall tales we tell – the lies, the porky pies, all those "you are my
soulmate, my other half, I'd never survive without you in my life",
even the "till death do us part" –

but it is rarely the case if we're totally honest, couples separate,
love is often lost along the way, yet, persistent,
we think we're different

sitting on the sofa, my blanketed legs over yours. We watch the news,
stories of bloody wars in a world gone crazy. Sounds of painful
partings. Families are ripped apart, parents are torn,

orphans are born, & you turn to me with a thought that remains
unspoken, forgotten between mind and mouth,
along with so much more.

Connections crumble though death is still our long-term project, for now
the parting has started, as you fade inside leaving me to fold
the blanket and turn off the TV.

Dear God,

i smell of burnt hairs
from seared images
on my brain's soft flesh
they won't go away

they play over and over
even behind closed eyes
day and night
like a broken record
someone's left spinning

dear god, fix my brain
turn it off so i don't hear
the 4am bang of his head
colliding with kitchen tiles

where i now stand
& see again the pool of blood
under him grow, hearing
my intake of breath so i am woken
over and over night after night

yet day after day we sit with morning coffee
at the table that broke his fall & his teeth
while he hides behind bandages
& forgets to take his meds

and i sound like a broken record
someone's left spinning & all

i want is to speak to the others
i passed on that PTSD path
our connected visions cry

dear god stop these images
our brains won't turn off
they play over and over day and night
like a broken record and we want

to wake & feel him/her/them
not this fear again and again
beside us on a soft bed of cool
sheets in a pool of moonlight
when we close our eyes to sleep

My Precious

Holding your cooling hand,
bedside, they said I had better

take your wedding ring
or it might get "disappeared"

its fading ghost now
a mere shadow on my finger.

So it hangs with mine –
twin markers round my neck –

chained together to show me
that time flows not in a line,

but in circles around scars
where pain won't bend.

And when I feel the ground shift,
like a rip curl pulling me down,

around and around,
and can't see the sky,

only taste salt water,
and can't breathe,

bursting for air
but feeling nothing there,

I slip my finger in it,
my precious, cold & smooth,

and you appear –
your hand in mine,

your fingers in hold, to squeeze,
to ground me with warm gold.

The Bike Lock

you did ask of course luv
before turning the screw
so tight there was no way in hell
it was ever coming off again:
is this the right spot?
are you sure this is what you want?
as you fixed the lock mount
at my requested odd angle
and I swung my leg over and
said *of course,* confident,
which is of course what I would say

now the lock mount
sits on the bar at that odd angle
where I can no longer get my leg over
which you would love to hear me say
laughing out loud at the innuendo,
which is of course
in this case just a bare fact
and so the mount
which was only meant as a temporary
fix has become permanent,
like you being gone

and of course
I cannot stop the clocks
or put out the stars, or ask you
to help me unhinge the moon
to get a leg over, proofread my poems,

my words in your mouth,
in a language where double meanings
can no longer find a space
and of course
that is the tragedy of it all being
so fucking permanent, not temporary

but let me be clear
this is not a poem about a lock
or even about fucking,
it is about your smile, your voice,
your hands, wanting to touch me,
to connect me to you, to everything
good, of course, being gone
and so my bike is proof
that Auden was right
about how funeral blues leave you
permanently at odd angles

bibliothèque intérieure

you wanted books in order
from a to z on the shelves
like a library, sorted;
me, by size or color or age

which you found so annoying
not grasping the logic
of a "little something"
so esthetic, so subjective

so now that i can do what i want –
mess them up, lay them upside down,
even on the floor under a cuppa,
whichever way, whatever order –

i don't … i can't –
& though you won't sigh & side
glance over my negligence
i keep your established plan

of bookshelves full of silent
words, sometimes highlighted
by your hand where they touched
you quietly, which i find

here and there, tucked away notes
like on the poem i wanted to use
for your ceremony, pulling it out
to find you speaking to me

Dear Rob,

I started to write to you
today. The pain gave way
to words, but gave no relief
and I know what they say
is: *That's how it goes with grief*!
but still I wish for another
conversation – it can be just
a short one. Some connection.
So I search, scrolling
through messages
trying to find traces
of your voice, of the "luv"
you had used to rename me
turning me into emotion –
of something to latch on to
even for the brief time of
a quick word still online
like the left over smell
of cinnamon in the kitchen
after baking, but there is
nothing there to peruse,
the deleted files and
archives of a past life
are empty. The smooth
tone of you gone, erased
all those meaningless voice
messages of *What's for dinner luv?*
Or *Two stops out on line 7 –*
crossing the river!

Or *Got some red wine*
but where's the corkscrew?
Or *My body misses your body*
Or *When are you home?*
Or *Where are you?*

The Dog Threw up on the Rug Again

Twice. That 3 o'clock brutal wake up that's
now two rings on the rug that will never fade
and I miss your skill, despite your deaf ear,

in steering her clear of the bed, the pillows,
or any fabric that kept the trace of her
delicate digestion with which we kept pace.

Now it's just me, down on all fours, wet rag
in hand, rubbing the floor and cursing the chore
that used to be yours, like so much more you
left behind – that space beside me in the bed,

where we used to lay like two commas on a sheet,
the place the dog now takes, all those signs
of you around the house where you left a mark
that I try to erase day by day, especially at 3am.

Falling/Fall In

I've still got your picture on the fridge.
Things slip through my fingers,
side glanced, when I pull them out,

like the ice tray, shattered cold
crystal and I'd like to be more
like those cubes and just let go –

falling without a care of where I
splinter into a million prisms
not be the one to pick up
the pieces or wipe the floor clean

below where you have your arm
around me with a smile on your face –
blue sky & colorful beach umbrellas
on the horizon of our summer holidays.

I decide instead to fall in love
with someone I can trust to see me –
a mirrored vision – not only pretty,

not in perfect shape, a bit too loud
and rough around the edges, who'd laugh
at a joke that wasn't one at the wrong

time, in the wrong place. So while I sink
in melting bath water and wait for wisdom
from the floating world to rise, I look
at the reflection & see my blurred body

under the surface, me
over her or her over me
at tangled angles and know
that love can just be to be.

Balloons and Flying Things

post-scriptum for him and her

I thought I saw her yesterday,
floating on a dying breeze
caught in the setting sun
flicking on and off in that horrid
metallic pink jumper
from her disco days
but then I lost her as I rounded
the corner heading home
only to see her again, deflated
and stuck at the top of a bare
tree, dressed in blue, waiting.

I thought I saw him yesterday,
flying in a murmuration
after the doctors said he would leave –
can something come too soon
and too late at the same time? –
he was reaching out
from his tethered bed
to catch what he saw
through clouded eyes
and left me here alone
looking up and waiting.

www.ingramcontent.com/pod-product-compliance
Ingram Content Group UK Ltd.
Pitfield, Milton Keynes, MK11 3LW, UK
UKHW041316190726
13845UKWH00025B/321

9 789363 543744